# Up and Under

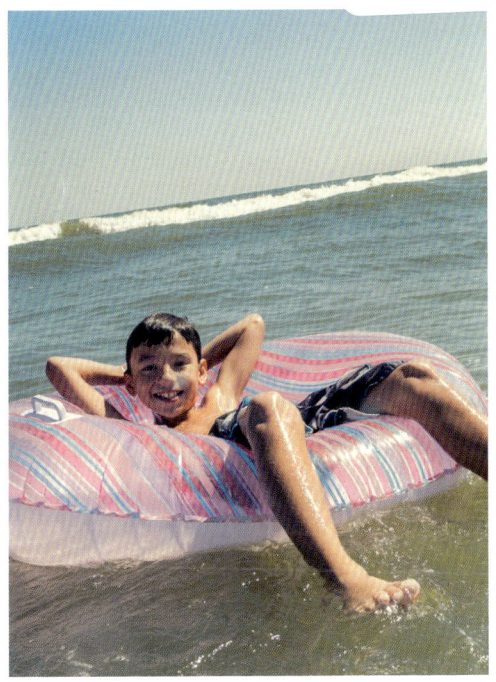

written by Rachel Walker

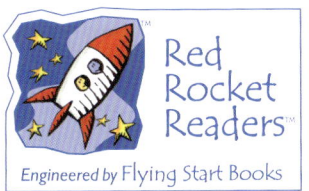

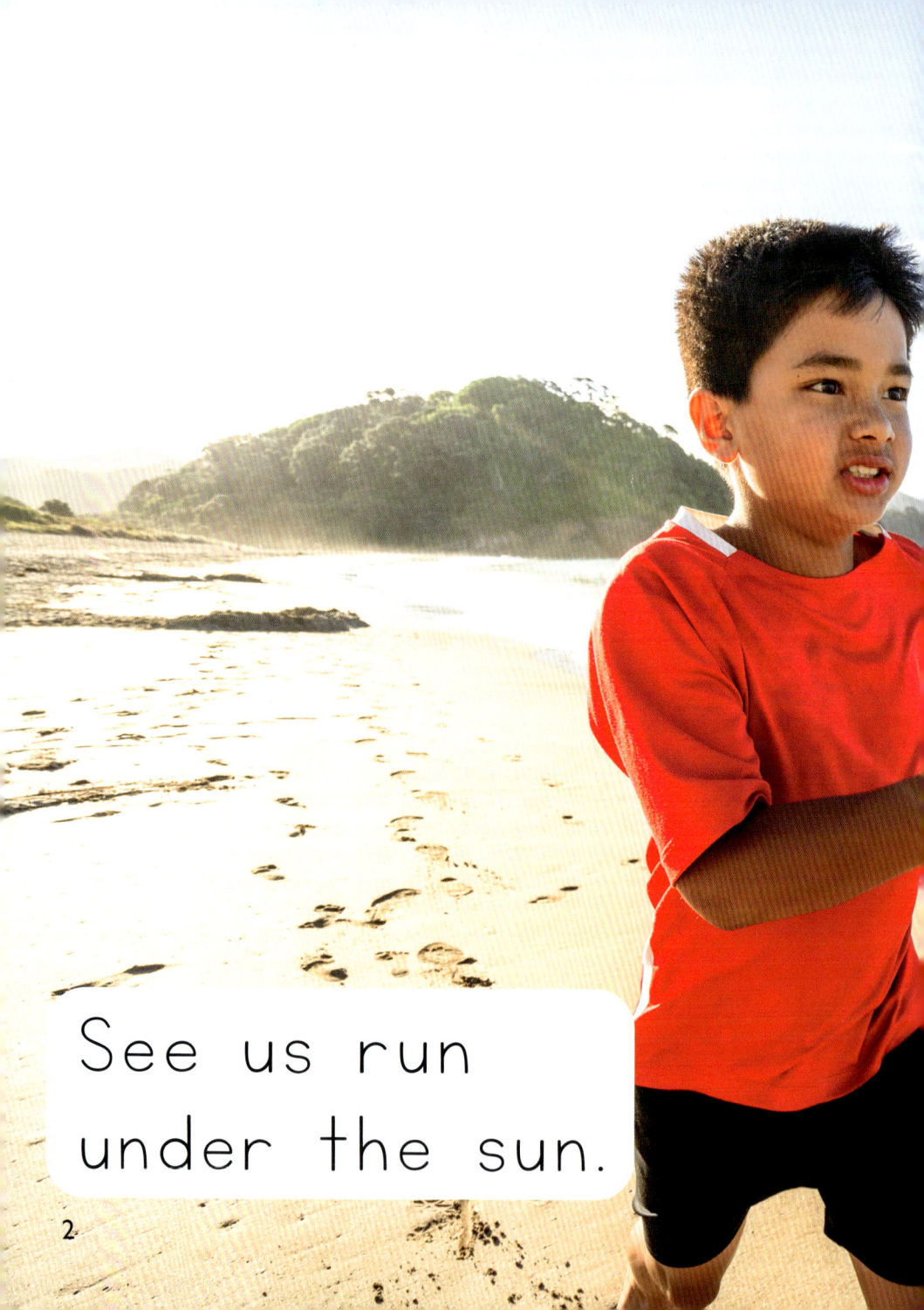

See us run under the sun.

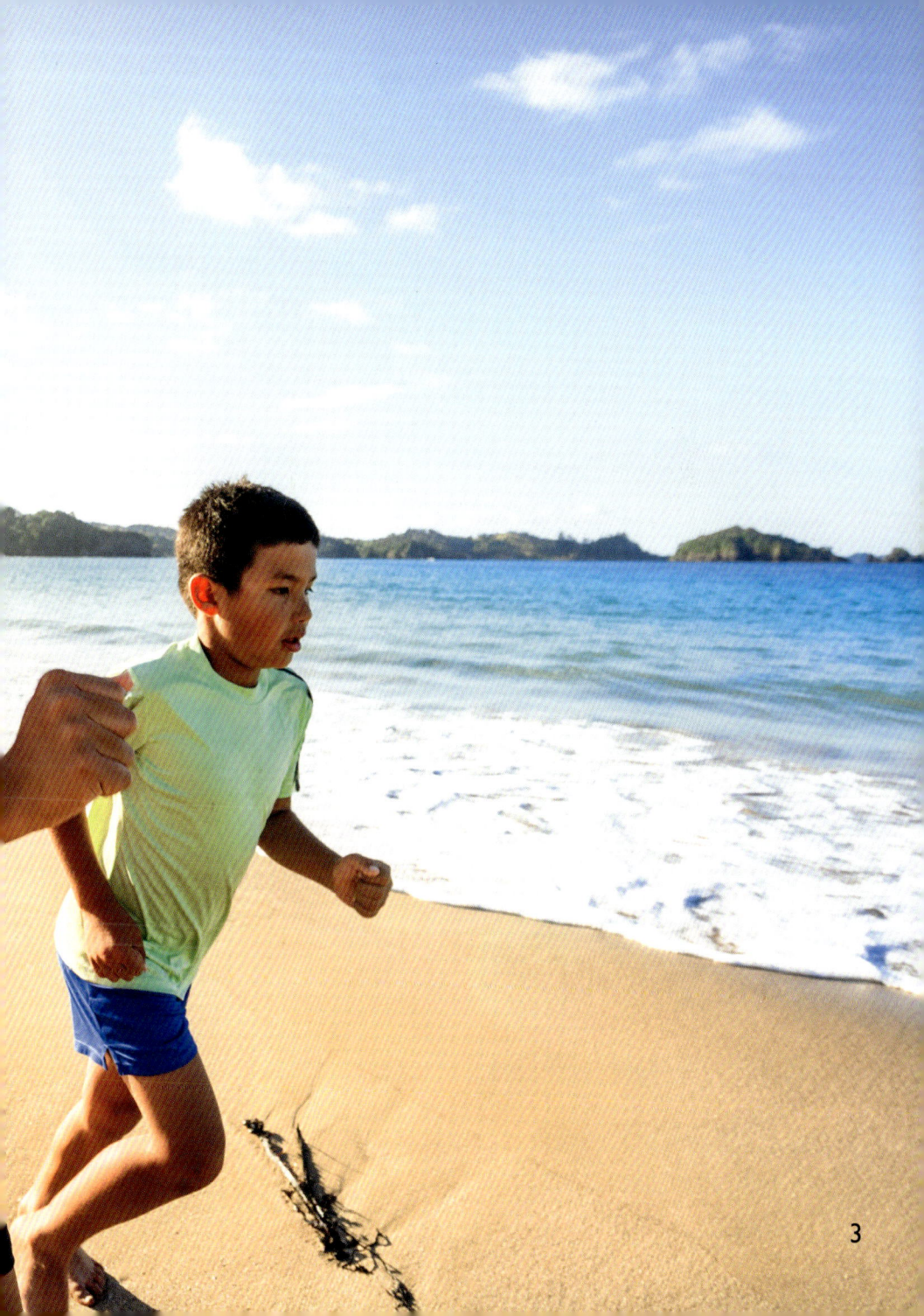

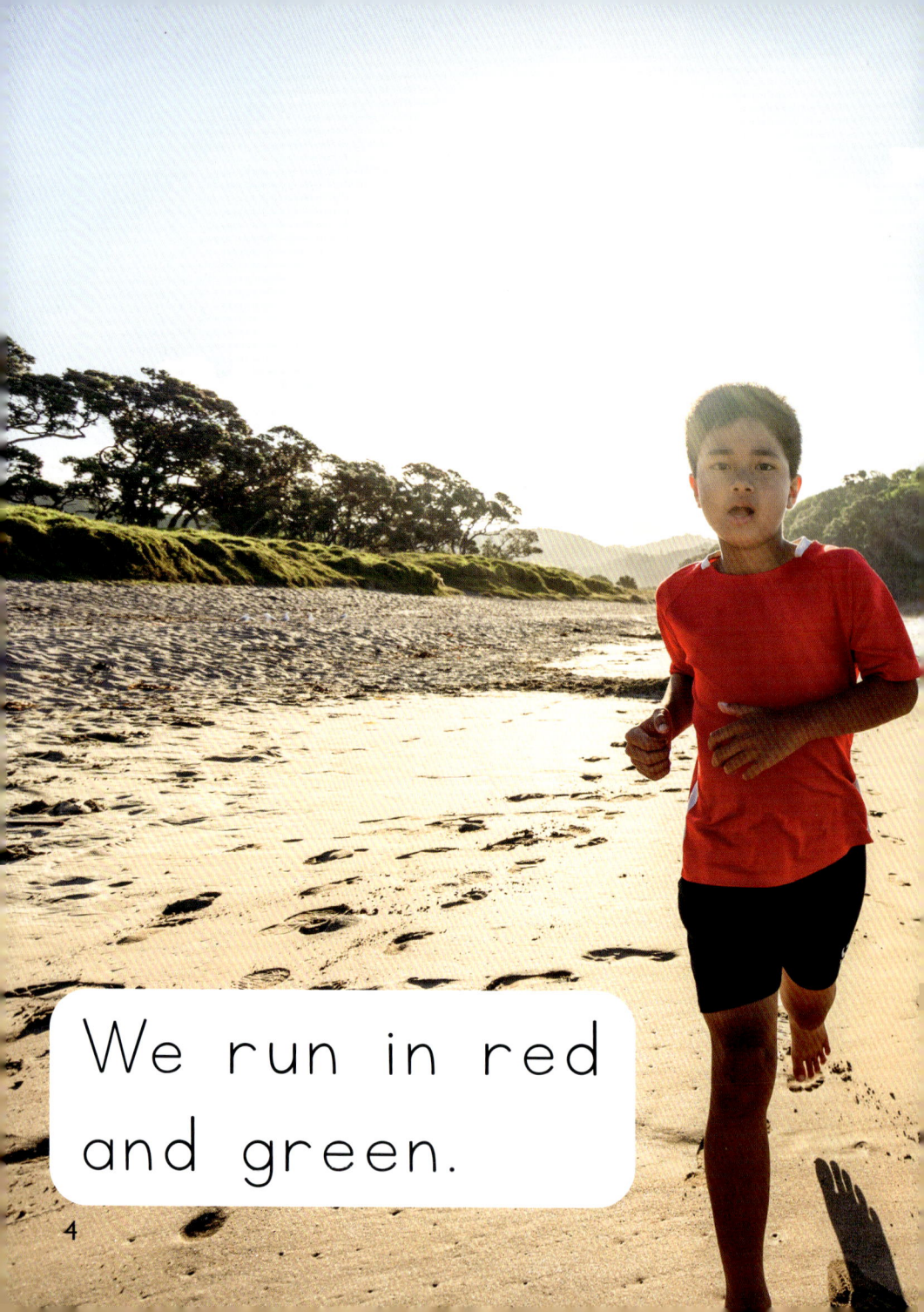

We run in red and green.

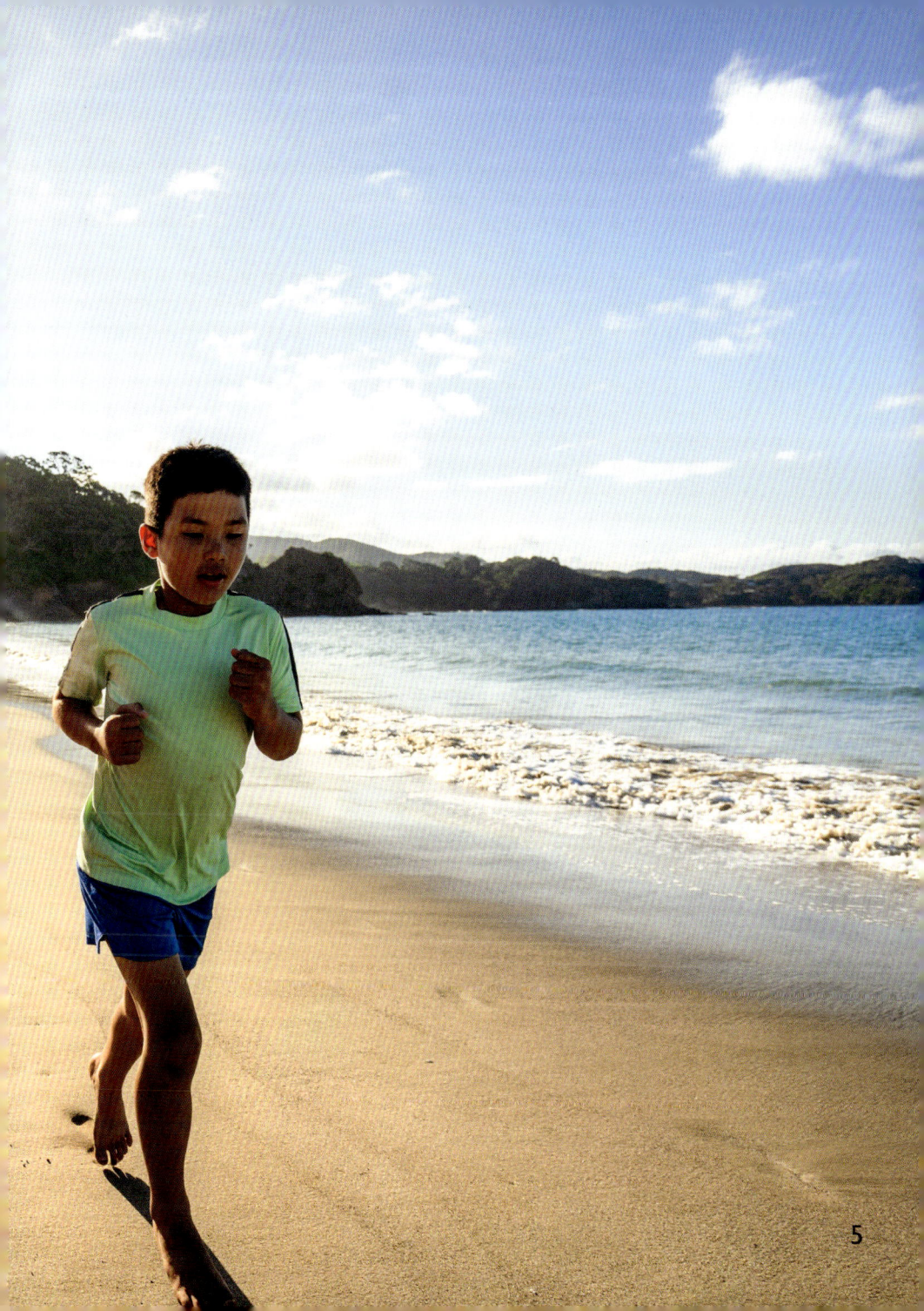

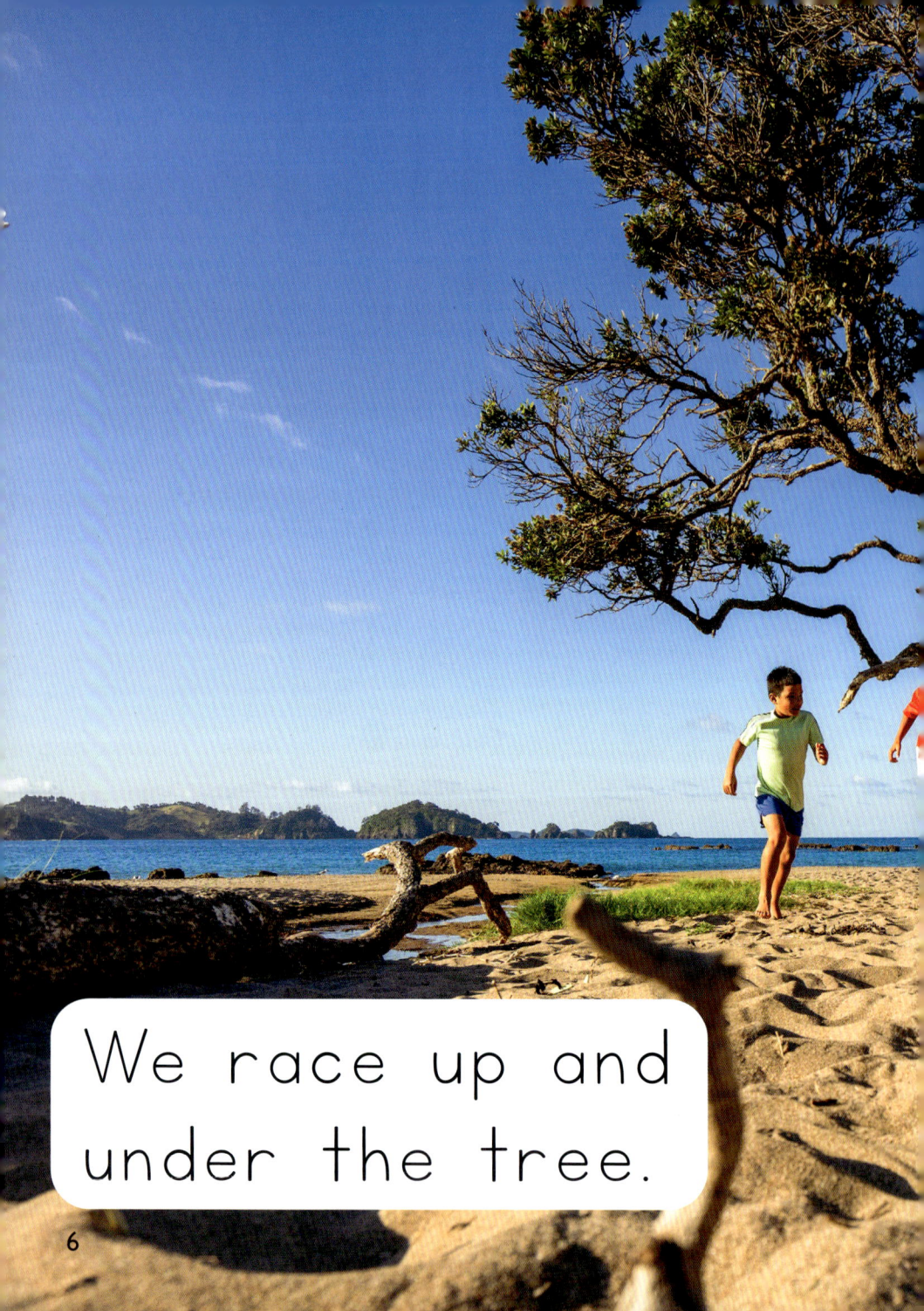

We race up and under the tree.

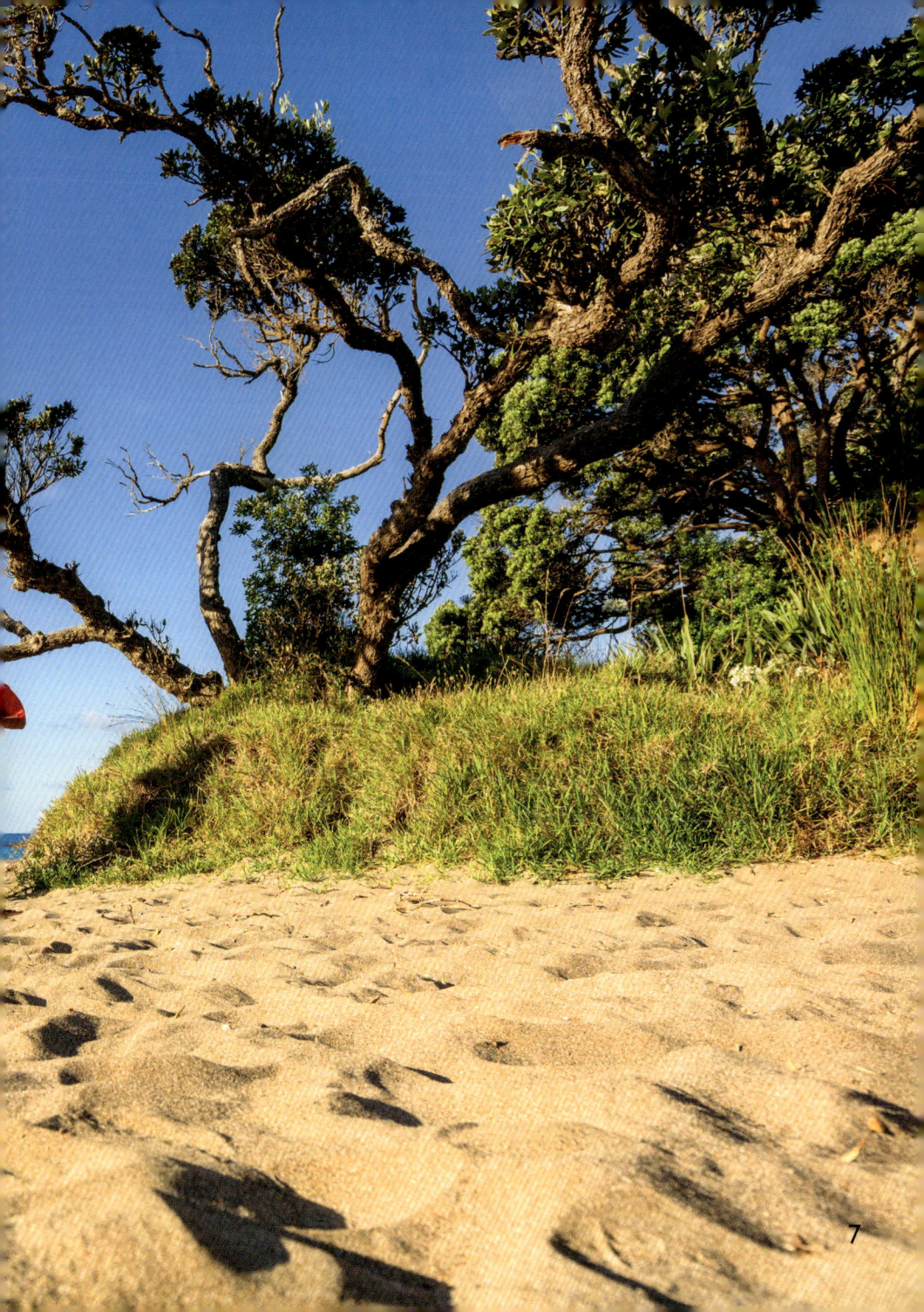

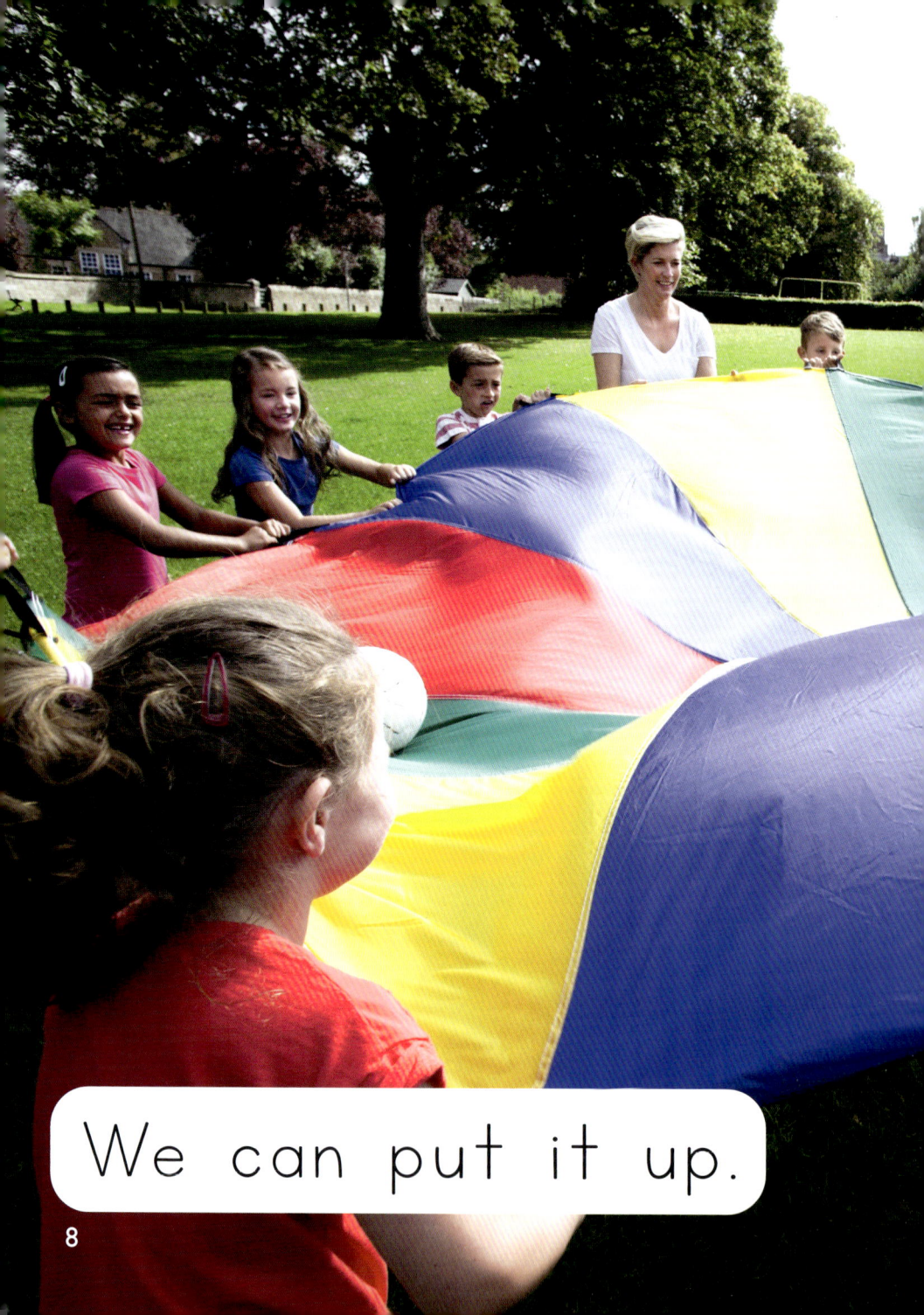
We can put it up.

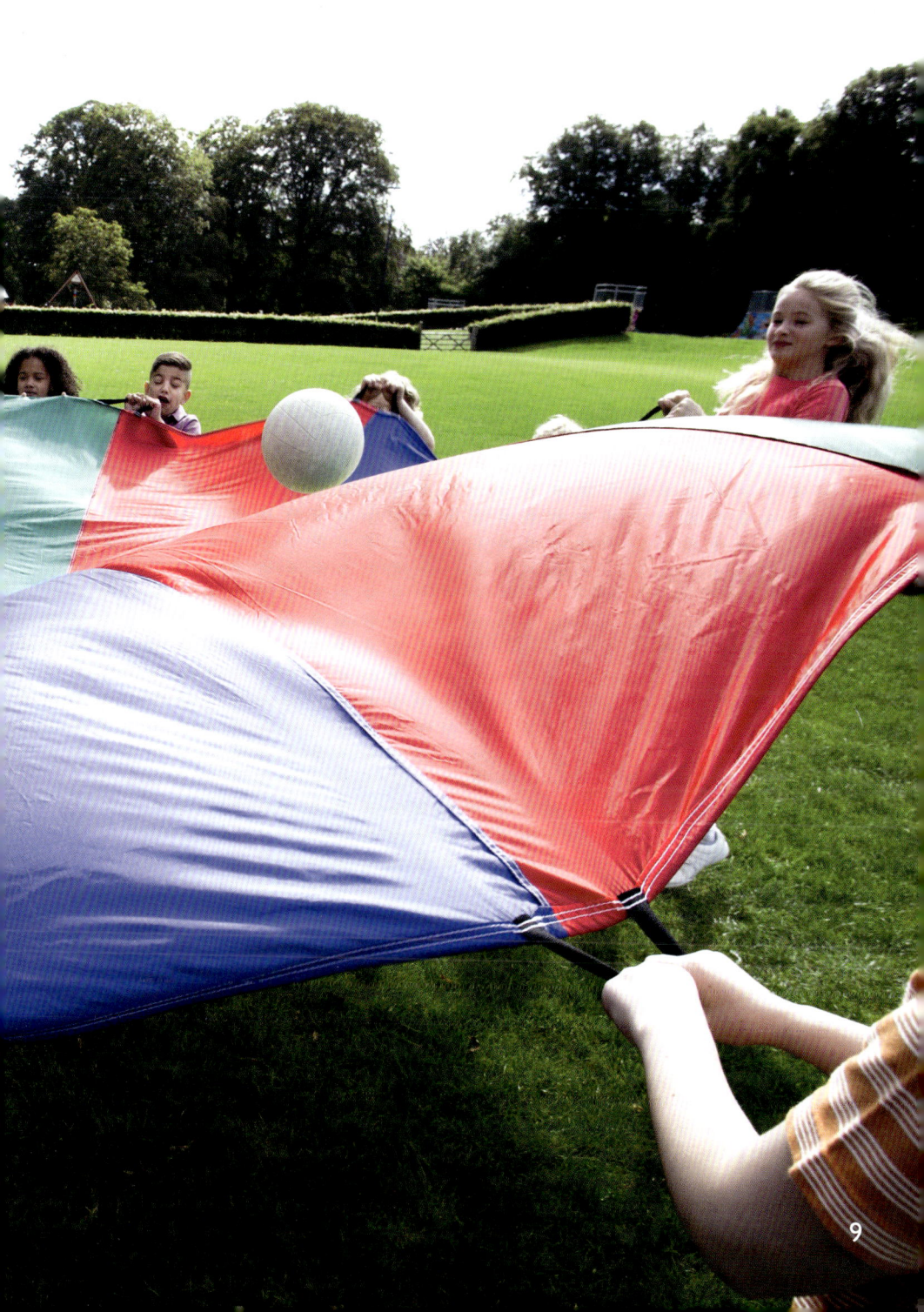

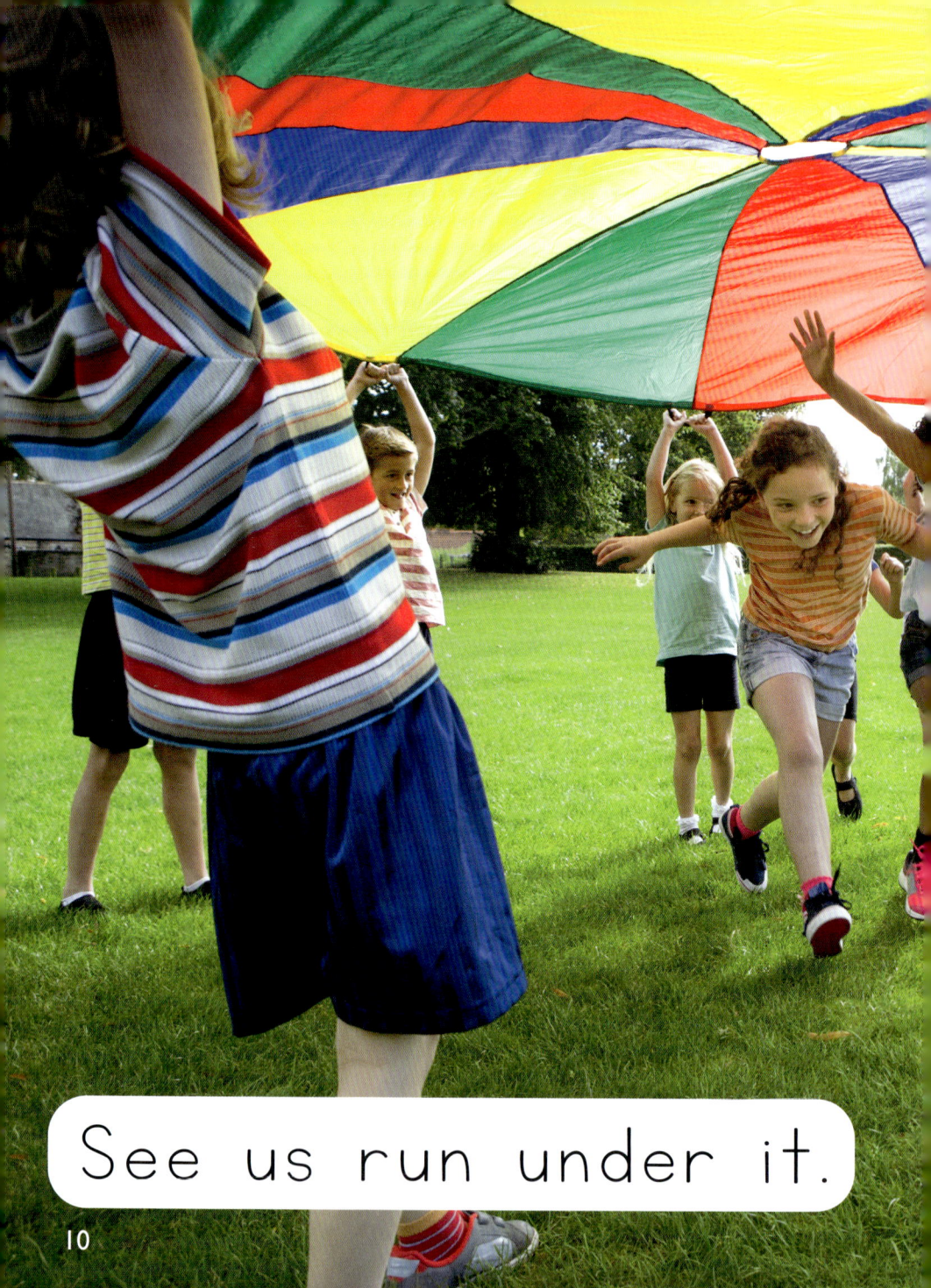

See us run under it.

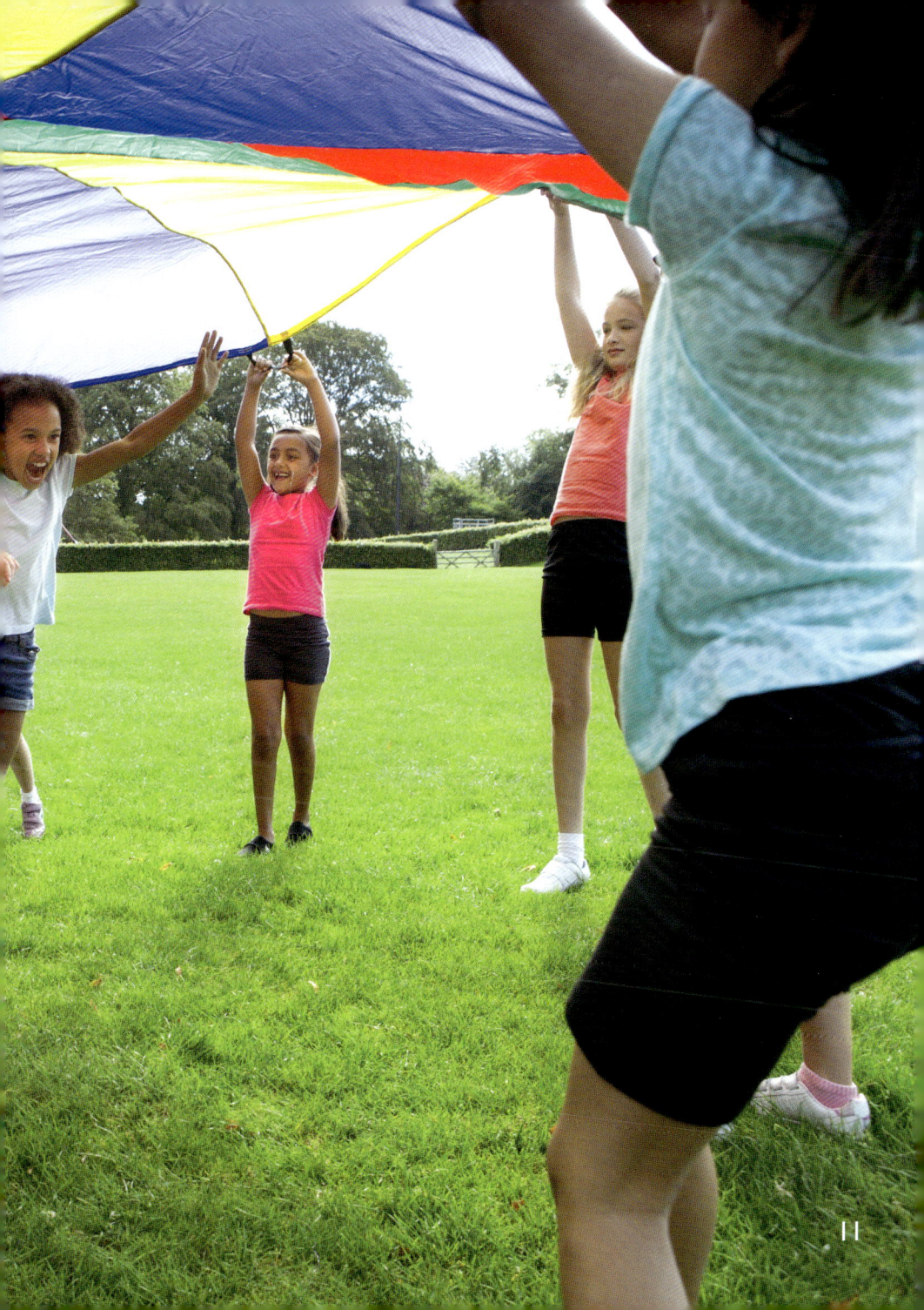

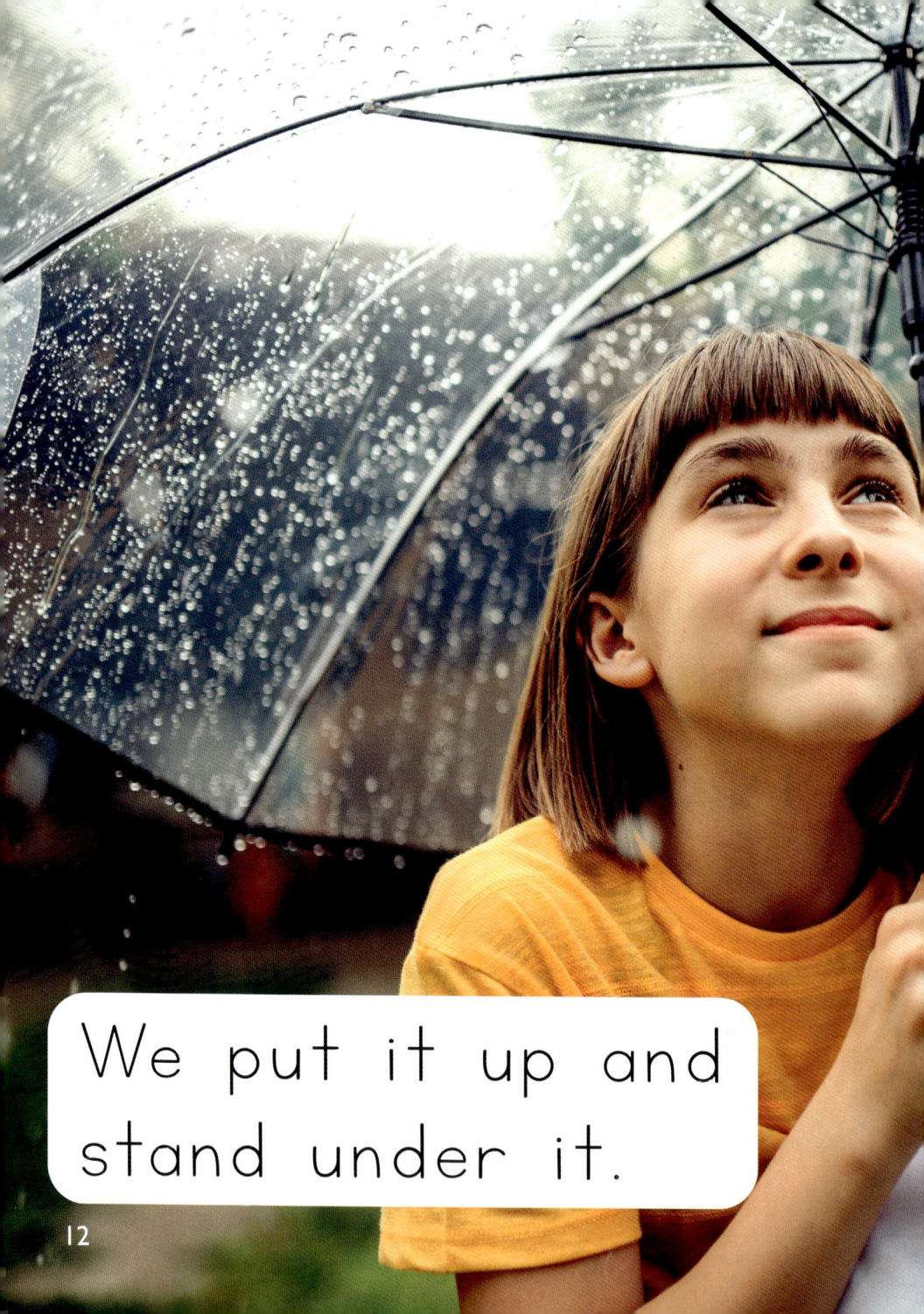
We put it up and stand under it.

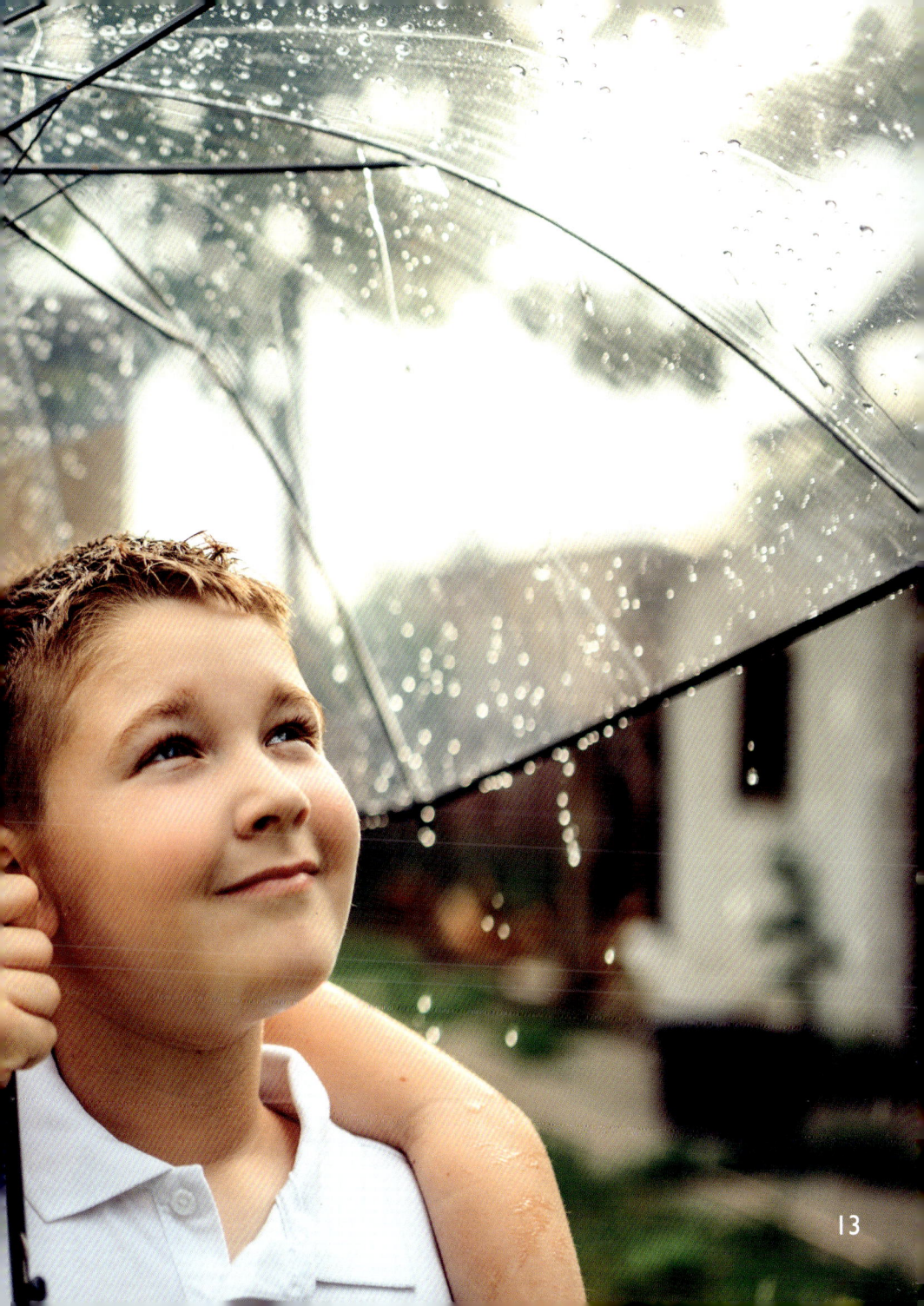

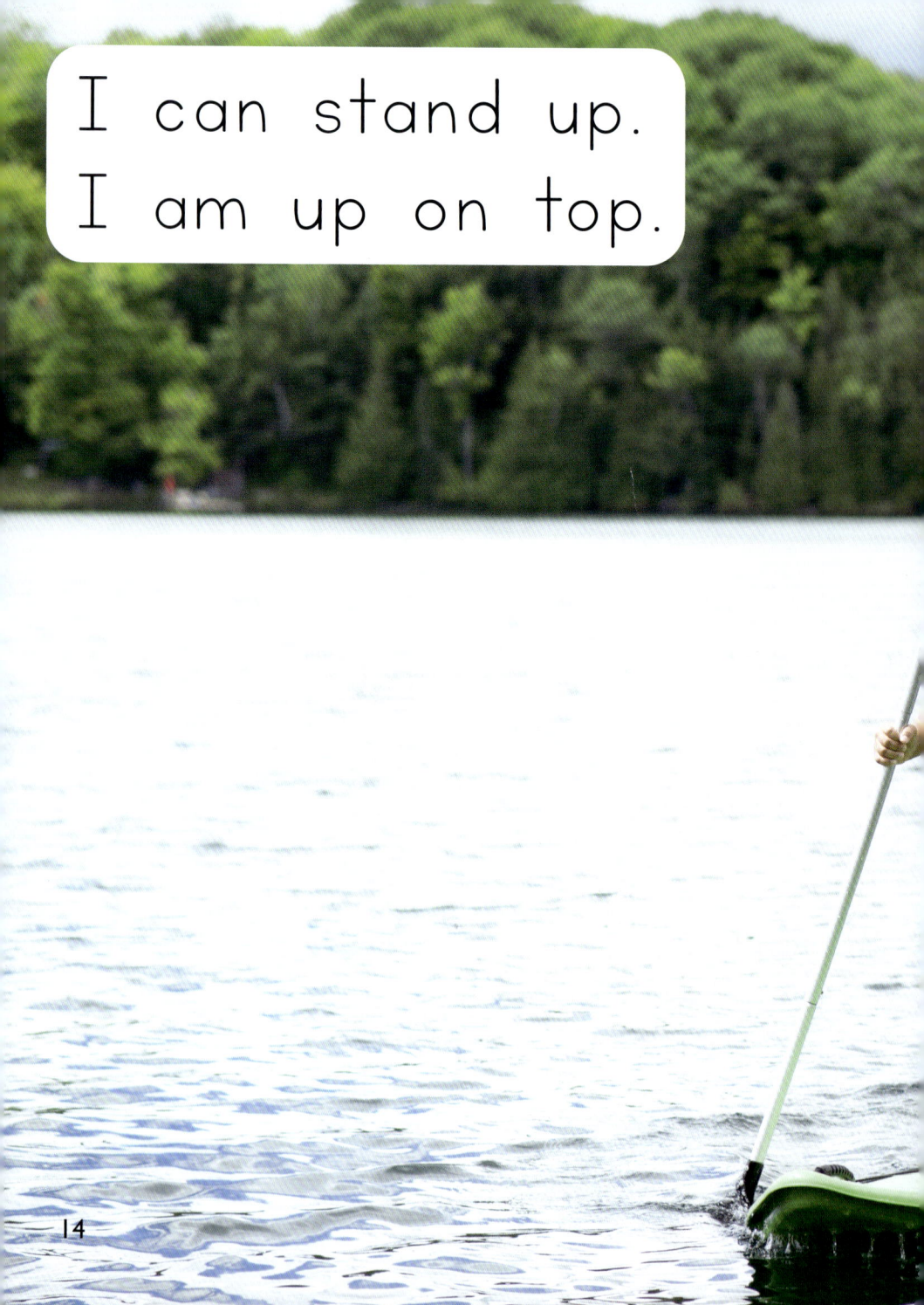

I can stand up.
I am up on top.

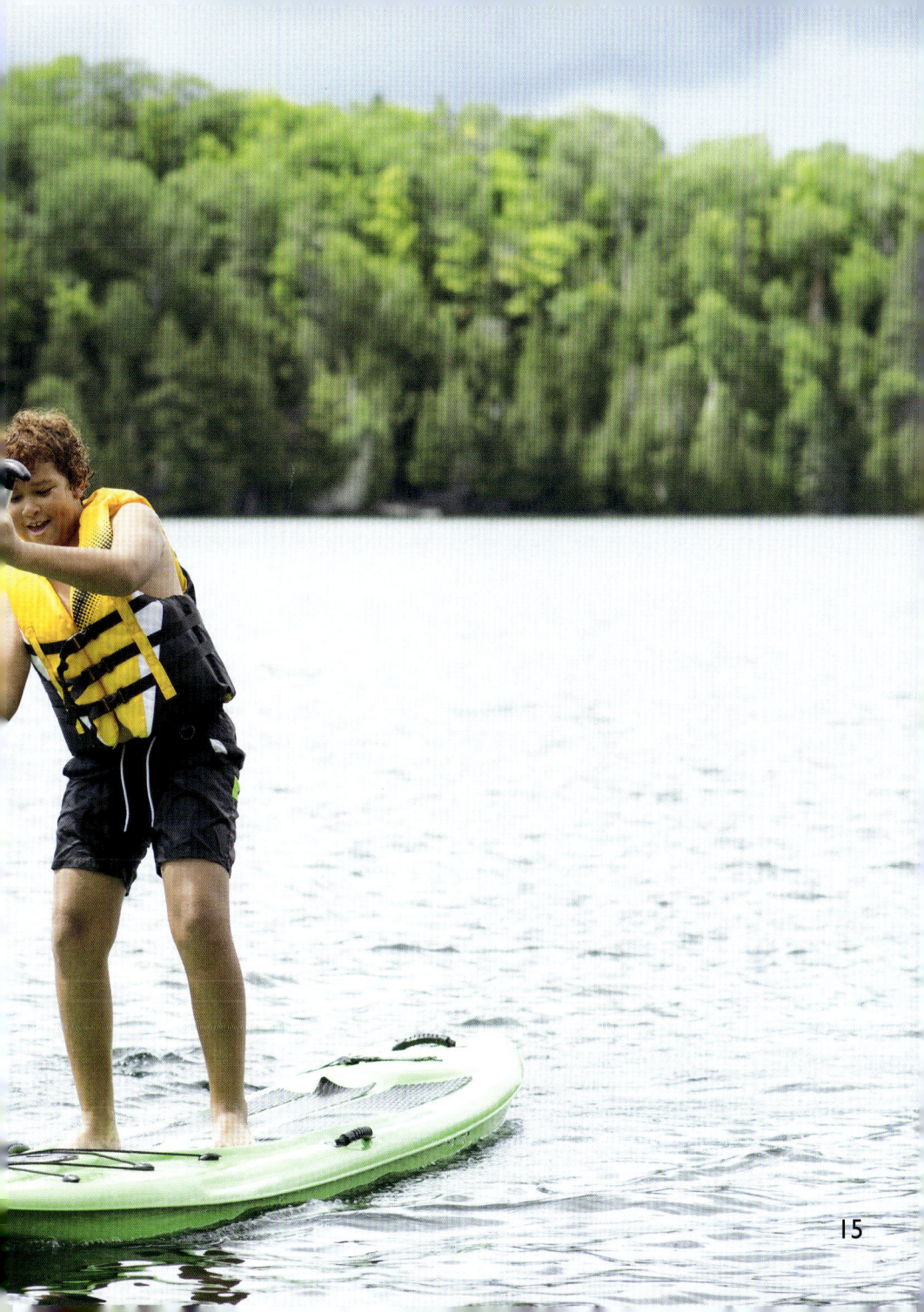

I sit and I rest.

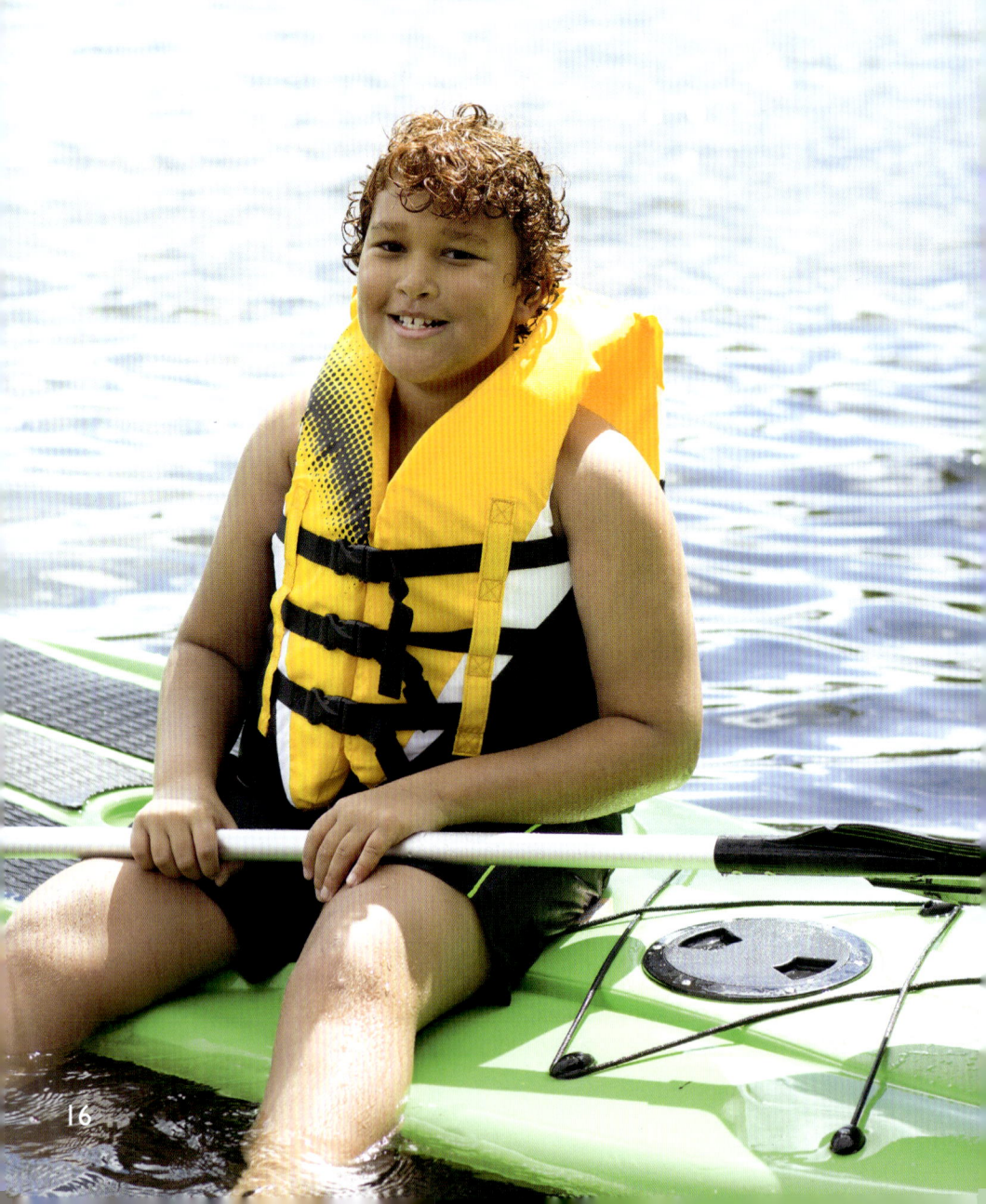